Contents

Any words appearing in the text in bold, **like this**, are explained in the Glossary.

What is a fox?

An adult fox is about the same size as a small dog.

A fox is a kind of wild dog. A fox has a bushy tail, large pointed ears and a long **muzzle**. The fox found in Britain is called the red fox.

Wild Britain

Fox

Louise and Richard Spilsbury

www.heinemann.co.uk
Visit our website to find out more information about **Heinemann Library** books.

To order:
☎ Phone 44 (0) 1865 888066
🖷 Send a fax to 44 (0) 1865 314091
🖥 Visit the Heinemann Bookshop at www.heinemann.co.uk to browse our catalogue and order online.

First published in Great Britain by Heinemann Library, Halley Court, Jordan Hill, Oxford OX2 8EJ, part of Harcourt Education Ltd. Heinemann is a registered trademark of Harcourt Education Ltd.

Editorial: Lucy Thunder and Helen Cox
Design: David Poole and Celia Floyd
Illustrations: Jeff Edwards, Alan Fraser and Geoff Ward
Picture Research: Catherine Bevan and Maria Joannou
Production: Séverine Ribierre

Originated by Dot Gradations
Printed and bound in Hong Kong, China by South China Printing

ISBN 0 431 03930 5 (hardback)
07 06 05 04 03
10 9 8 7 6 5 4 3 2 1

ISBN 0 431 03937 2 (paperback)
08 07 06 05 04
10 9 8 7 6 5 4 3 2 1

British Library Cataloguing in Publication Data
Spilsbury, Louise and Spilsbury, Richard
Fox. – (Wild Britain)
599.7'75'0941
A full catalogue record for this book is available from the British Library.

Acknowledgements

The Publishers would like to thank the following for permission to reproduce photographs:

Ardea p8 (John Daniels); BBC p20; FLPA pp4, 15, 22, 23 (Terry Whittaker), 5 (Hugh Clark), 10, 13 (Robert Canis), 19 (R Bird), 29 (Silvesteis); Natural Science Photos p27 (Paul Hobson); NHPA pp9 (Michael Leach), 12 (Hellio and Van Ingen), 17 (Laurie Campbell), 21 (Andy Rouse), 28 (Derek Karp); Oxford Scientific Films pp6 (Hans Reinhard), 25 (Mike Birkhead); RSPCA pp11 (William S Paton), 14 (Robert Glover), 16 (Vanessa Latford), 24 (Ron Perkins), 26 (Andrew Linscott); Windrush Photos p18 (David Tipling).

Cover photograph of a fox, reproduced with permission of NHPA (Laurie Campbell).

The Publishers would like to thank Michael Scott for his assistance in the preparation of this book.

Every effort has been made to contact copyright holders of any material reproduced in this book. Any omissions will be rectified in subsequent printings if notice is given to the Publishers.

A male fox (right) is called a **dog fox** and a female fox (left) is called a **vixen**.

Red foxes have bright, rusty red or orange-red fur. They usually have blackish legs and white fur on their belly. **Male** foxes and **female** foxes look similar.

5

Where foxes live

This fox lives in a woodland habitat.

Foxes live wherever they can find food and somewhere to hide. In Britain, foxes live in all kinds of **habitats**. They live in woodlands, hills, **estuaries** and sand dunes.

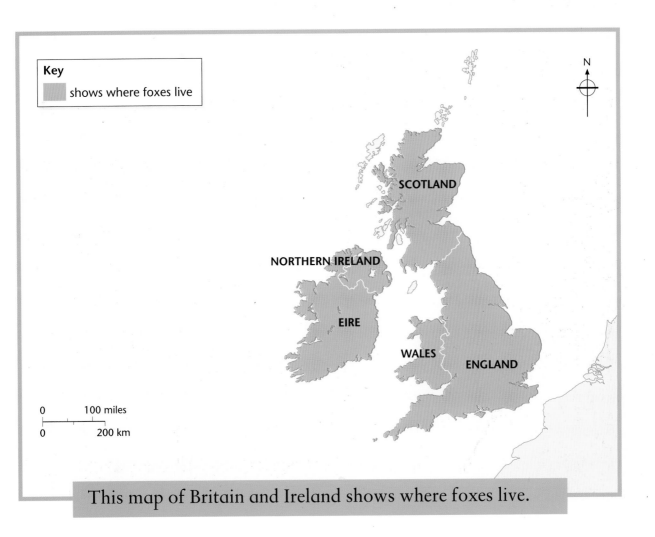

This map of Britain and Ireland shows where foxes live.

Foxes also live in and around towns and cities. They hide in quiet places like the edges of parks, churchyards or near canals and railway lines.

What foxes eat

Foxes mostly eat other animals, but they sometimes eat plant roots or berries.

Foxes eat almost any animal they can catch, including rabbits, birds, frogs, mice, earthworms and beetles. They also eat any dead animals that they find.

This fox is finding something to eat in a dustbin.

Foxes that live in different **habitats** eat different things. Those living by **estuaries** eat crabs and dead seabirds. Town foxes eat household scraps, such as meat bones.

Finding food

This fox is pouncing on a mouse that it has crept up on.

Foxes are mainly **nocturnal**. That means
they usually come out in the evening or at
night to find food. They creep up silently on
an animal, then run up and pounce on it.

Foxes have such good hearing they can hear a mouse squeak from over 30 metres away!

Foxes usually hunt alone. They find animals using their eyes and their very good hearing and **sense** of smell. They have sharp front teeth for catching food.

On the move

Foxes often have to run as fast as they can to catch a meal.

Foxes trot and walk on all four legs. They can also swim well when they have to. Most foxes carry their tails straight back when running. The tail droops when the fox walks.

Foxes often use the same paths to move around their territory.

Foxes usually move around in one area. This is called their **territory**. They stay in this area so they know it well. They know the best places to find food and good places to hide.

Sleeping and resting

Foxes usually rest in the shelter of a hedgerow or among grass, like this.

All animals need to rest or sleep. Foxes mostly rest during the day and hunt at night. They usually sleep on the ground in a place where they cannot be seen easily.

Foxes often sleep like this, with their tail over their nose and front paws.

Sometimes there is not much cover to hide in or the ground is very wet. A fox may sleep in a hole in the ground or in a hollow tree.

Fox families

Male and female foxes mate in winter. Baby foxes are born about two months later.

In winter **male** and **female** foxes come together to have babies. They **mate** and then a baby fox begins to grow inside the female.

Foxes often make an earth near water so the female does not have far to go to drink.

Before the **cubs** are born, the foxes look for a place to make an underground den. This is called an **earth**. It is where the female will have the cubs.

A fox's earth

This fox is digging out an earth.

Foxes sometimes dig out the soil to make
an **earth** for themselves. They often move
into an old rabbit or badger's hole and
make it bigger.

This earth entrance has fox droppings and food scraps outside, so there are probably foxes inside.

An earth usually has more than one entrance. Behind each entrance there is a tunnel that leads to a hole about 1 metre wide. This is where the **cubs** will be born.

Young foxes

The cubs are born furry and helpless. At first they cannot see, hear or walk.

A **vixen** gives birth to her **cubs** in spring. She has four or five cubs in a **litter**. The cubs feed by drinking milk from their mother.

The **dog fox** may bring food for the mother while she is in the earth with the cubs.

The vixen stays in the **earth** with the cubs for the first two or three weeks. After three weeks she visits the earth at night to feed the cubs. She rests elsewhere in the day.

Growing up

This cub is asking an adult to cough up some chewed food for it to eat.

At three weeks old the **cubs'** eyes are open and they can walk. They leave the **earth** at five weeks old. They eat soft meat that their parents have chewed for them.

Most young foxes leave the family when they are grown up.

The cubs stop drinking milk at seven weeks old. They eat chewed meat until they are four months old. They then learn how to hunt. By autumn they are fully grown.

Sounds and smells

Adult foxes call loudly to tell each other where they are.

Foxes tell each other things using lots of different sounds. For example, **cubs** yelp to call their mother when they do not know where she is. **Vixens** bark if they are angry.

This fox can tell that this area belongs to a different fox, because it can smell the other fox's urine on the ground.

Foxes also use smells to pass messages to each other. Foxes spray strong-smelling **urine** around the edge of their **territory**. This tells other foxes to keep away.

Dangers

Some people use traps, or snares, like this one to catch foxes. This is because foxes kill their hens or young lambs.

Sometimes foxes kill hens that belong to farmers. Some people hunt or shoot foxes to stop them taking farm animals.

Most foxes live to about two or three years old. A few reach ten years old.

When people build houses in the country, foxes may lose their homes. The foxes have to move to find new places to live or new kinds of food to eat.

A fox's year

When the cubs come out of the **earth** in April or May, they play in the warm spring sun.

Foxes do things at certain times of the year because of the changing **seasons**. **Cubs** are born in spring when the weather is getting warmer and there is most food.

A fox's summer coat makes it look thinner and long-legged.

Adult foxes **moult** in summer. They lose their hair and grow a new coat. At first the new hair is short and cool. By winter, it grows thick again to keep them warm.

Animal groups

Scientists group together animals that are alike. Foxes are in the same group as dogs and wolves. All three have long legs, long sharp front teeth and a long **muzzle**.

fox

dog

wolf

The artwork on this page is not to scale.

Glossary

cub young fox

dog fox male fox

earth name for the underground den foxes have their babies in

estuary coastal area where a river meets the sea

female animal that can become a mother when it is grown up. A female human is called a woman or a girl.

habitat natural home of a group of plants and animals

litter set of babies

male animal which can become a father when it is grown up

mate what a male and female animal do to start a baby growing inside the female

moult when an animal loses its old coat of hair ready to grow a new one

muzzle nose and mouth on an animal such as a fox or a dog

nocturnal being active at night and resting during the day

scientist person who studies the world around us and the things in it to find out how they work

seasons the year is divided into four seasons – spring, summer, autumn and winter

senses most animals have five senses – sight, hearing, touch, taste and smell

territory an area of land where an animal spends most of its time

urine proper name for wee

vixen female fox

Index